JUL 1 2 2022

P9-CJJ-264

My First Book of
Chinese Calligraphy

text by **He Zhihong** and **Guillaume Olive**

illustrations and calligraphy by **He Zhihong**

TUTTLE Publishing

Tokyo | Rutland, Vermont | Singapore

"Books to Span the East and West"

Tuttle Publishing was founded in 1832 in the small New England town of Rutland, Vermont [USA]. Our core values remain as strong today as they were then—to publish best-in-class books which bring people together one page at a time. In 1948, we established a publishing office in Japan—and Tuttle is now a leader in publishing English-language books about the arts, languages and cultures of Asia. The world has become a much smaller place today and Asia's economic and cultural influence has grown. Yet the need for meaningful dialogue and information about this diverse region has never been greater. Over the past seven decades, Tuttle has published thousands of books on subjects ranging from martial arts and paper crafts to language learning and literature—and our talented authors, illustrators, designers and photographers have won many prestigious awards. We welcome you to explore the wealth of information available on Asia at **www.tuttlepublishing.com**.

Published by Tuttle Publishing, an imprint of Periplus Editions (HK) Ltd.

www.tuttlepublishing.com

English translation copyright © 2022 Periplus Editions (HK) Ltd.
Copyright © 2006 Editions Philippe Picquier

Library of Congress Control Number: 2010928296

ISBN 978-0-8048-5516-7

Distributed by

North America, Latin America & Europe
Tuttle Publishing
364 Innovation Drive
North Clarendon, VT 05759-9436 U.S.A.
Tel: 1 (802) 773-8930;
Fax: 1 (802) 773-6993
info@tuttlepublishing.com
www.tuttlepublishing.com

Asia Pacific
Berkeley Books Pte. Ltd.
3 Kallang Sector #04-01
Singapore 349278
Tel: (65) 6741 2178
Fax: (65) 6741 2179
inquiries@periplus.com.sg
www.tuttlepublishing.com

First edition
24 23 22 21   6 5 4 3 2 1

Printed in China   2110EP

TUTTLE PUBLISHING® is a registered trademark of Tuttle Publishing, a division of Periplus Editions (HK) Ltd.

To Cathy

Contents

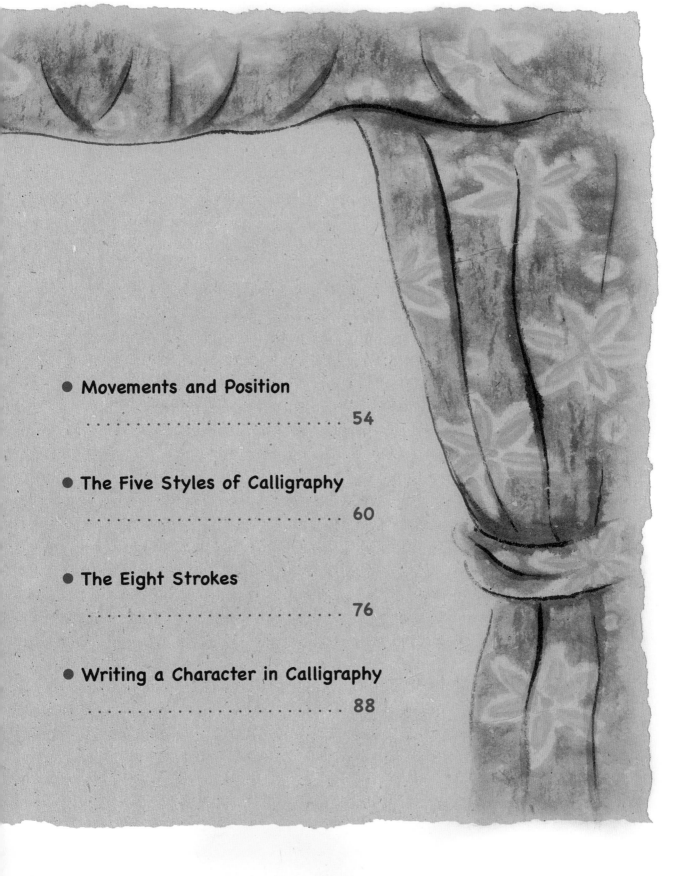

"My name is Mimi, I'm eight years old, and I'm learning Chinese calligraphy!

Chinese writing and calligraphy are two different things. People often confuse the two. Kids in China learn to write with a pencil or a pen, but they don't all practice calligraphy—you use a brush for that. Calligraphy is the art of creating the characters beautifully, not just writing them down. In China it's been an art for thousands of years, and it's still very important today. Just like famous paintings, wonderful Chinese calligraphy can be displayed in museums and can be very valuable.

Together we'll start by discovering the rules of Chinese writing... which are very different from our English writing rules. Then we'll learn about the important ideas in calligraphy, and finally we'll practice. As you'll see, it's not so hard. While you learn calligraphy, you'll discover some other special talents too: how to master your mind's focus, your breathing, and even how you move!

But first, let's uncover the mysteries of Chinese writing, from its beginnings...**"**

The Evolution
of Chinese Writing

According to legend, there was once an extraordinary being whose name was Cang Jie. He had two pairs of eyes. One day, while observing animal tracks on the ground, he copied them and got the idea of writing. That's how he invented Chinese characters.

Did you know the Chinese language has no alphabet? Chinese characters are not letters, but drawings. Chinese writing is one of the most ancient systems of writing in the world. It appeared about six thousand years ago, on pottery, when messages were painted and carved onto the clay.

Slowly, writing evolved. That means it developed and got more complicated over time. At first writing was carved on turtle shells and animal bones, then later it was carved on bronze and stone. Characters were of different sizes and there were many versions of the same word. But around the year 200 B.C.E., the ruler nicknamed "the first emperor," Qin Shihuang, united the whole country and made rules to follow about the way to write each character. Also, after paper was invented, using a brush to write became common.

Century after century, Chinese characters have evolved in different styles that you'll learn about later in this book. In 1956, China simplified many of the characters by reducing the number of strokes they had.

Chinese writing is made up of around 10,000 characters. In order to read the newspaper, you have to know 3,000.

Look how the Chinese characters have evolved, from the way they were written thousands of years ago to the way we write them today:

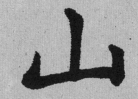

Three peaks standing in the sky represent the shape of a mountain…

…yes, you're right! This character means "mountain"!

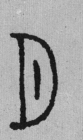

An outline that stretches its arm forward is…

a person!

This one is easy, like a letter D, but since you know that there's no alphabet in Chinese: what looks like a "D"?

It's the moon!

A curving line that flows along,
with dots beside it like drops
or banks of a river is…

water.

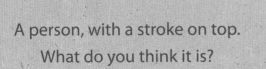

A person, with a stroke on top.
What do you think it is?

It's the sky!

Now it's your turn! Guess which character goes with each drawing, and write it in the correct box. (Answers start on page 16.)

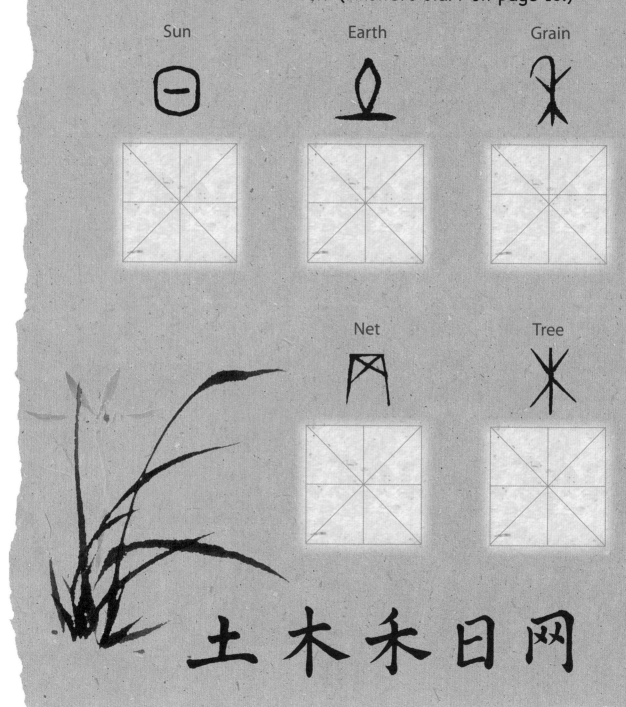

Sun

Earth

Grain

Net

Tree

土木禾日网

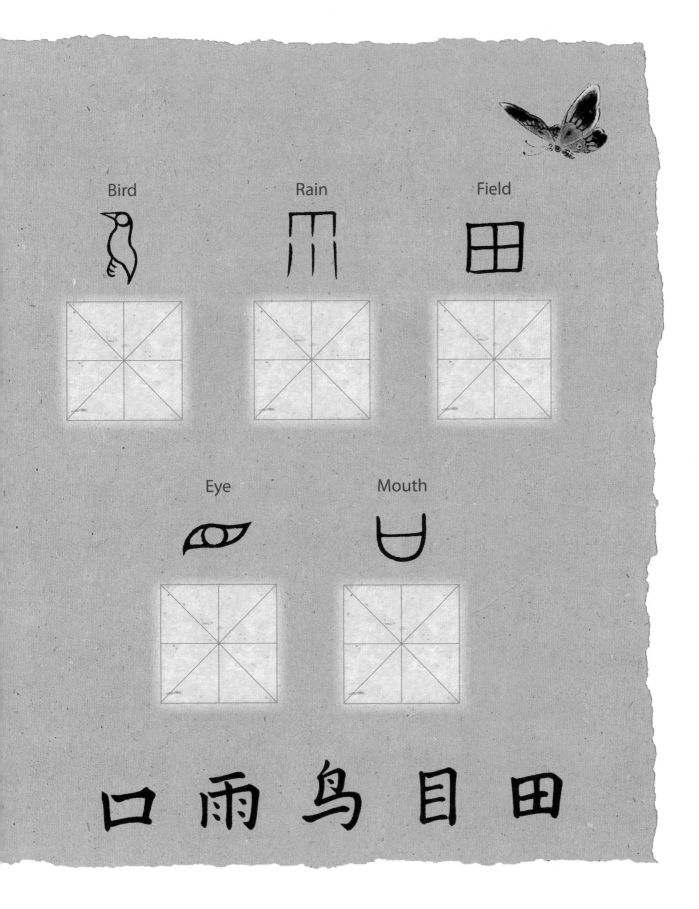

Bird

Rain

Field

Eye

Mouth

口 雨 鸟 目 田

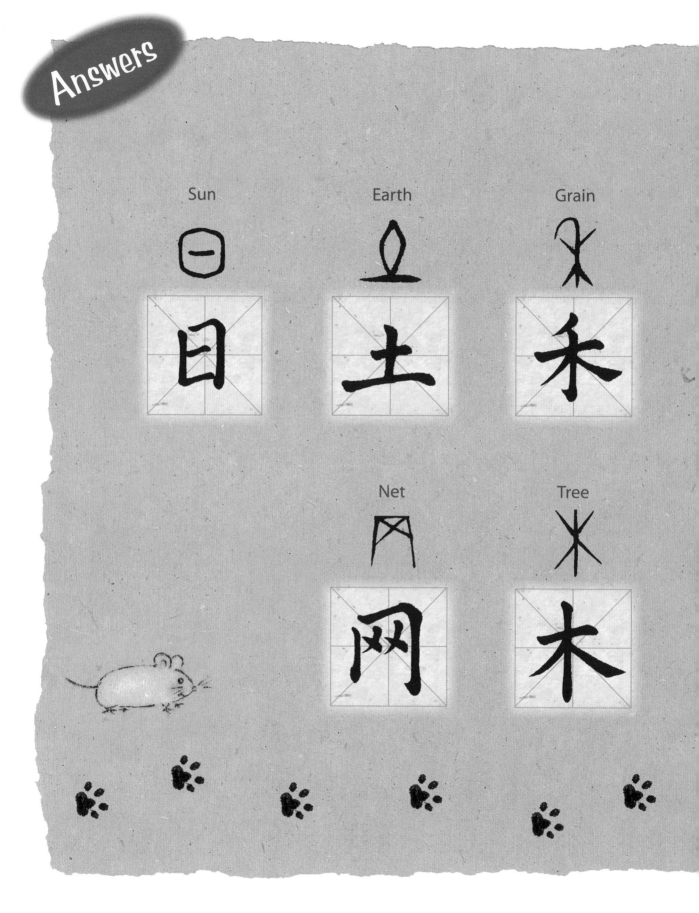

Sun

Earth

Grain

Net

Tree

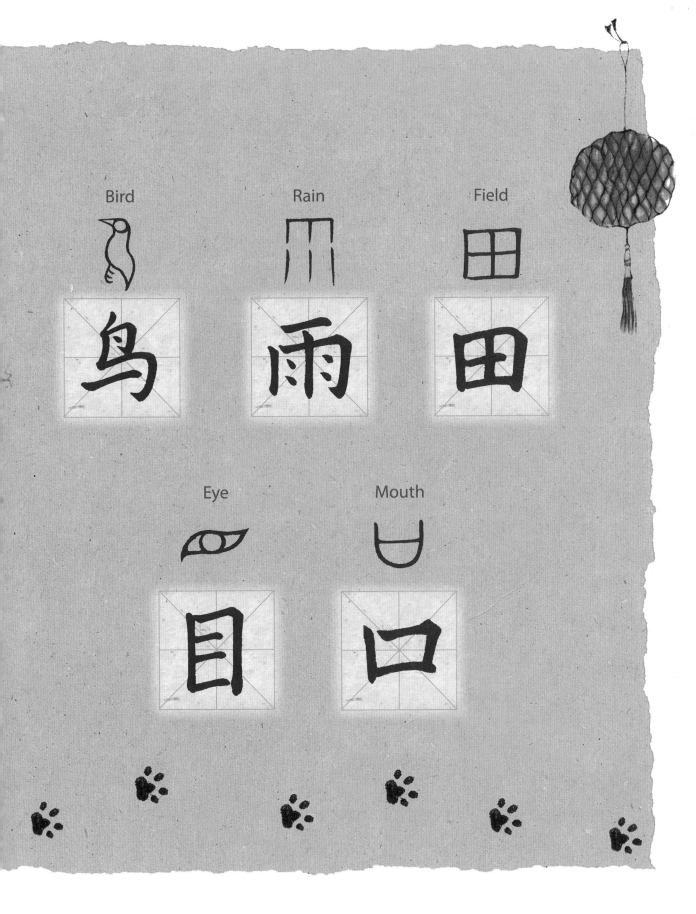

Bird

鸟

Rain

雨

Field

田

Eye

目

Mouth

口

一

The Order of the Strokes

二

The characters are made up of strokes. There can be just one single stroke, or as many as thirty! But beware: you have to write each one of them in a special order.

From top to bottom

Vertical ("up and down") strokes are written from top to bottom. When a character is made up of several parts, some placed on top of others, you begin with the top ones, and finish with the bottom ones.

Look at this character. It means "two."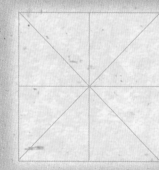

To write it, first write the top stroke, then the bottom stroke.

From left to right

Horizontal ("across") strokes are written from left to right. When a character is made up of several parts, some placed next to others, you begin on the left and finish on the right.

To write "person," 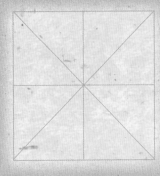 first write the left stroke, then the right stroke.

First middle, then left, then right

When a character is made up of a vertical center part with two symmetrical parts on each side, first you write the center part, then the left part, then the right.

Look at the character for "water": 水

To write it, start with the center stroke, from top to bottom, going up a little at the end to make the little hook. Then add the left stroke and then the right stroke, being careful to write them so that the character looks balanced on both sides.

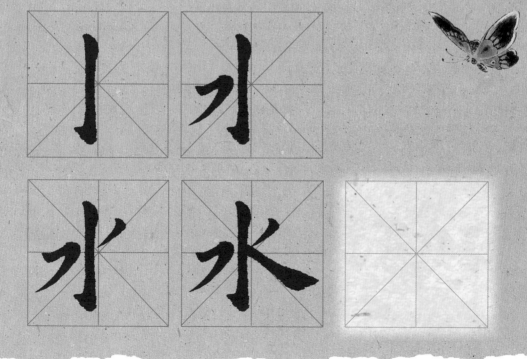

First horizontal, then vertical

When a horizontal stroke crosses a vertical stroke, first you write the horizontal stroke, then the vertical stroke.

The number "ten" looks like a plus sign: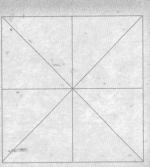

First write the horizontal stroke, from left to right, then the vertical stroke, from top to bottom.

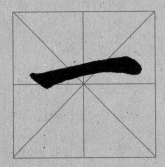 

When a horizontal stroke is at the very bottom, you write it after the vertical stroke.

Look at the order of strokes to write "insect":

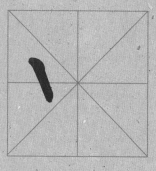 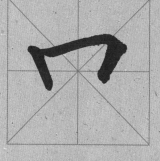 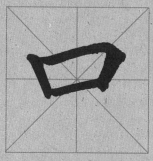

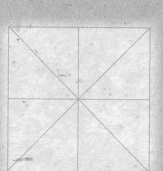

From outside to inside, then the closing

When a character is made up of a frame that "closes in" one or more parts, first you write the frame, then the parts contained inside, and finally the base of the frame. You do not close the box before filling it!

Here is an example: "field."

Start with the left stroke, from top to bottom. The second stroke draws the frame. Then fill the inside, with the horizontal stroke, then the vertical stroke. Now you can close the box!

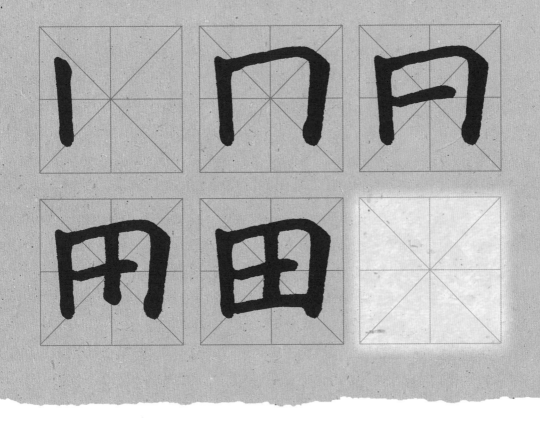

When a character has a dot on the top right, that dot is usually written last.

That's what happens with "dog."

犬

Sun

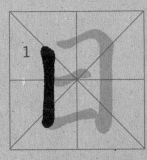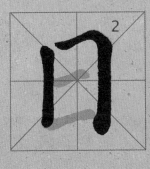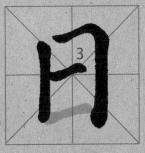

Rest

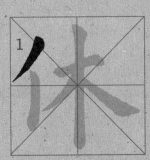

Tea

You can see that each character, no matter how many strokes, fills the exact same space, like it's in an imaginary box always of the same size.

Nowadays, sentences are written across, from left to right. But Chinese used to be written in columns, from right to left.

Your turn! Write these characters, remembering to be careful to follow the correct order of strokes:

Water

Sky

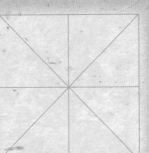

Character

字

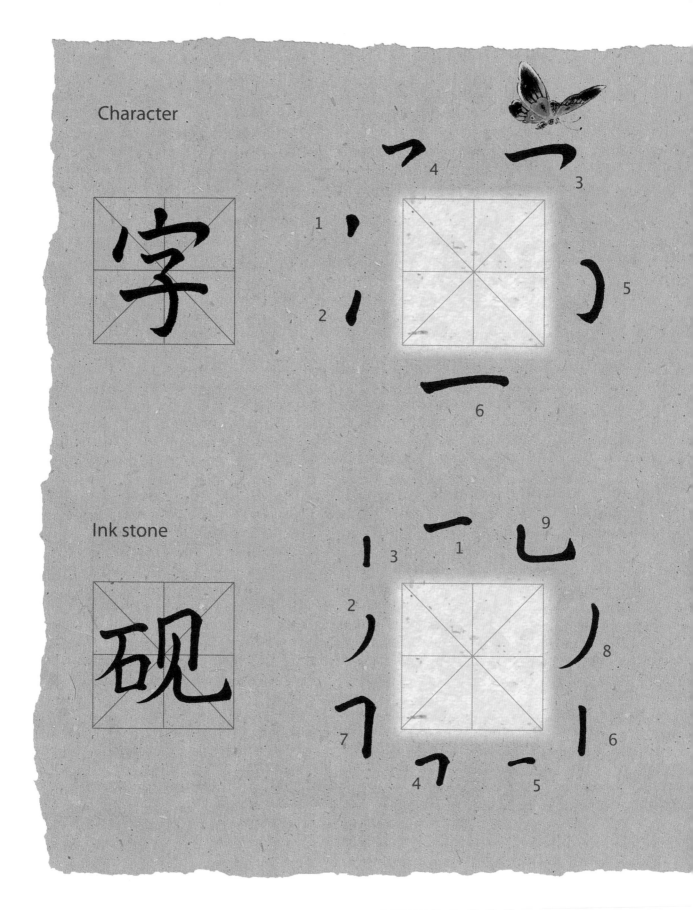

Ink stone

硯

Tiger

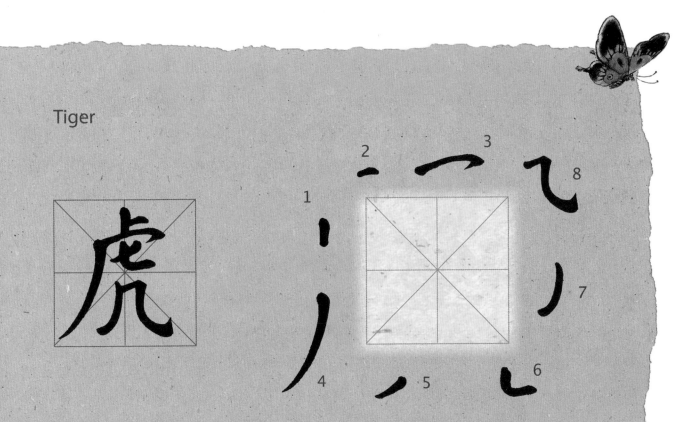

Now that you know the proper order of strokes, you can write all the characters without making any mistakes! It's true, some look really complicated. But you'll soon notice that many characters have certain key parts that always look the same, and are easy to spot: those are the "radicals."

人

The Radicals

众

Most characters are made up of different parts, like jigsaw puzzle pieces. Among these parts, there are the radicals. There are about 200. Radicals give clues about the meaning of the characters. For instance, characters that contain the **tree** radical all have a relationship to trees: root, pine tree, forest, fruit...

Radicals can be written in different ways in order to fit better with the character. For example, the **person** radical can be written like the character for "person":

人

...or instead, it can look like this:

亻

And in the same way, the **water** radical can be written like the character for "water":

水

but also with three dots that resemble drops.

氵

That's how the jigsaw puzzle works: by combining a radical with one or more other parts, you get a new word!

The **person** radical + "tree": this character means "rest"!

$$ 亻 + 木 = 休 $$

The **water** radical + "eye": you have "tears"!

$$ 氵 + 目 = 泪 $$

So the radicals are a very handy tool to help you memorize the characters: you will more easily remember a character if you can remember its radical.

Each radical is placed at a specific spot. For example, the three-dot **water** radical is always on the left side of the characters; the **roof** and **grass** radicals are on top.

Here are several examples
to help you understand how
the characters are made up:

Person + person = follow
radical

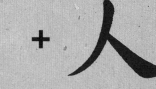 +

Person + two people = crowd
radical

 =

Person + tree = rest
radical

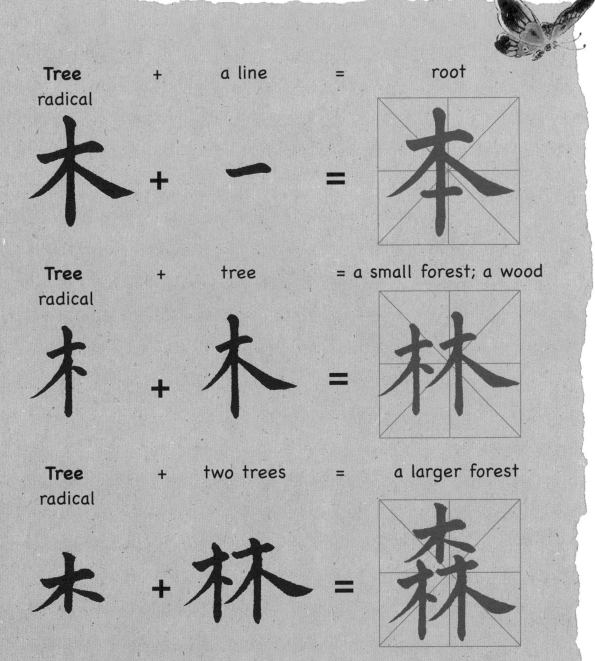

Tree radical	+	a line	=	root
木	+	一	=	本

Tree radical	+	tree	= a small forest; a wood
木	+	木	= 林

Tree radical	+	two trees	=	a larger forest
木	+	林	=	森

Did you notice something? The more parts in a character, the smaller they get. That's because each character always fits into an imaginary square that takes up the same amount of space, no matter how complicated the character is.

Your turn! You can practice making characters by joining together a radical and another part. Check out these examples, then add the correct radical in each box on page 39.

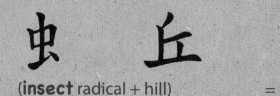

(**insect** radical + hill) = earthworm

(**field** radical + force) = masculine

(**stone** radical + little) = sand

(**sun** radical + moon) = light

丘
Earthworm

力
Masculine

石
田
虫
日
少
Sand

月
Light

心　亡　忘
(**heart** radical + flee)　= forget

火　火　炎
(**fire** radical + fire)　= burning

氵　目　泪
(**water** radical + eye)　= tears

女　子　好
(**woman** radical + child)　= good

艹　田　苗
(**grass** radical + field)　= sprout

山　丘　岳
(**mountain** radical + hill)　= high mountain

火
Burning

目
Tears

亡
Forget

子
Good

田
Sprout

丘
High mountain

女 山 艹 火 心 三

41

亻　山　仙

(**person** radical + mountain)　= immortal

囗　人　囚

(**enclosure** radical + person)　= imprison

宀　女　安

(**roof** radical + woman)　= quiet, peaceful

口　犬　吠

(**mouth** radical + dog)　= to bark

日　青　晴

(**sun** radical + blue or green color)　= beautiful

足　失　跌

(**foot** radical + losing)　= to trip, lose your footing

扌　石　拓

(**hand** radical + stone)　= enlarge

山
Immortal

人
Imprison

石
Enlarge

女
Quiet; peaceful

犬
To bark

青
Beautiful

失
Trip, lose your footing

口

日 足 扌 亻 山 口

Here is a list of the radicals we've seen:

Person 亻   Enclosure 口

Tree 木   Grass 艹

Field 田   Mountain 山

Stone 石   Water 氵

Insect 虫   Roof 宀

Sun 日   Mouth 口

Woman 女   Foot 𤴓

Heart   心   Hand   扌

Fire   火

Now that you know the key
ideas of Chinese writing, we
can begin learning calligraphy!

The Four Treasures
of Calligraphy

In China, calligraphy is an art, and calligraphers pay particular attention to the quality of their tools. There are four essential tools. They are called "the four treasures of the scholar's desk":

Paper

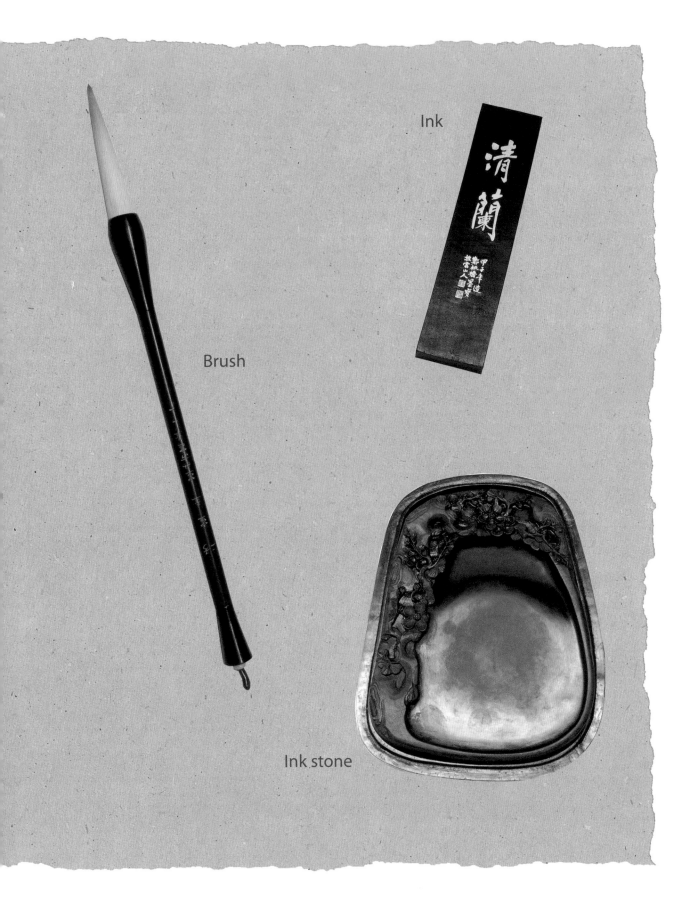

Ink

Brush

Ink stone

Did you know that paper was invented in China 2,000 years ago? It is said that a minister named Cai Lun invented paper after he observed wasps making their nest out of bamboo fibers. By crushing bamboo slats with water, Cai Lun created a paste that, when it dried, became a sheet of paper.

Chinese paper is sometimes called "rice paper," but it's not made out of rice! Most often it's made of sandalwood bark, mulberry fibers, or bamboo. Depending partly on what they're made of, different papers absorb more or less water. For example, tree-bark-based paper absorbs more than paper made from bamboo. That makes a difference in how calligraphy looks on the paper.

Chinese ink is made of soot from pine branches, or soot from the oil of the abrasin tree. The soot is mixed with glue and herbs. The mix is molded into small sticks, and dried. The ink sticks might be decorated with gold drawings or characters. Ink sticks are rubbed against the ink stone with a little water, to make liquid ink. (You can also buy liquid ink already made, in bottles.)

The ink stone is a special slab made of stone. It has a small pool carved into it. You pour a little water into it, and then you rub the ink stick against the stone to make liquid ink. The best ink stones have a rough texture good for grinding, and they produce a smooth and beautiful ink.

There are ink stones in all shapes and sizes. Their edges or lids are sometimes sculpted and decorated; some look like dragons or animals.

Besides helping to make ink, the ink stone also comes in handy when you want to get rid of extra ink on your brush, or to "sharpen" the point of your brush when you want to make special lines.

The brush is made from animal hairs glued into a handle, which is usually made of bamboo. Each kind of brush hair gives you a different kind of line, and feels different to use. The most common brushes are made of hare, weasel or goat hairs. The hare and weasel hairs are stiff, but the goat hairs are soft.

To do their job for you, brushes must be well cared for. After each time you use them, rinse them, blot them dry, and if possible, hang them with the bristles facing down. Don't let them soak in water too long or they could fall apart!

Along with the Four Treasures, you'll see other things on a calligrapher's desk too. You might notice brush holders, containers to rinse brushes, a thick felt mat placed underneath the paper, paper weights to hold edges down, seals for stamping your name in red ink, and so on. All these items are special and can be hard to find. But don't worry, you can start with plain paper (newsprint is good to use, because it absorbs water well), brushes that you already have, and black paint or bottled ink.

Movements
and Position

To practice calligraphy, you have to be calm and in a good mood! You also must be properly set up. Here's how.

First choose a well-lit place, and make sure you have enough room on your table. A chair without arms is best. Place your tools next to the hand that holds the brush, and place the sheet of paper in front of you.

Good posture is important. Sit up straight, with your feet flat on the ground. Your back must not rest against the chair, and your belly should not touch the table. You can use your fist to measure the correct distance between your belly and the edge of the table.

Next, place your arms on the desk, in line with your body. Get used to your work-space. Take a few deep breaths. Relax your arms, shoulders, and body.

To start, dip your brush into the water, then dry off the extra. Use your finger to check how moist the bristles are, and to make sure that the end is pointy.

Put a few drops of clean water in the ink stone, then hold the ink stick very straight, its end flat on the stone.

Rub the stick evenly against the stone, at a steady speed, to make liquid ink.

The brush must be held straight up and down. Follow the drawing:

Hold the brush between your thumb and pointer finger, with the middle finger a little lower. Use your pinkie and ring finger to push the brush toward the other side.

Make sure to keep your hand relaxed while it holds the brush. Put your other hand at the side of the sheet of paper.

Now you can dip your brush in the ink and experiment, to get used to everything. Make some lines, just to see how the brush and the ink act on your sheet of paper. Try brushes of different sizes, and try dipping them in more or less ink.

And before you write your first character, look at the different calligraphy styles with Mimi!

The Five Styles of Calligraphy

During the long history of China, the writing tools changed. And sometimes people needed to simplify some characters or to write more quickly. This is how the five different calligraphy styles were born.

川 ¹ 水 ² 水 ³ 水 ⁴ 水 ⁵

1. Zhuan Shu: The Seal Style

This is the most ancient style, going back over three thousand years! Its characters often look like drawings. It combines several kinds of writing from long ago, during the time of the First Emperor of China, for example the "Great Seal" style (*da zhuan*) and the "Small Seal" style (*xiao zhuan*).

It is still used in the carving of seals.

A seal is a stamp, often made of stone, where your name or special mark is carved. You use it to mark your "signature" on your work.

2. Li Shu: The Clerical Style

This is also called the "Chancery Style." It shows the change from the ancient forms of the characters, to their modern forms. It is easier and quicker to write than the Seal Style.

3. Kai Shu: The Regular Style

This is also called the "Normal Style" or "Square Style." It is the style used the most, and the one that is the easiest to read, since you can clearly see every stroke. You start learning calligraphy by practicing in this style.

4. Cao Shu: The Cursive Style

Here the strokes are all linked together, so the brush almost never leaves the paper. That makes the characters harder to read. This style is also called "fast" or "free style." Some calligraphers write so quickly in Cursive Style that they have to leave out some strokes!

5. Xing Shu: The Running Style

The Running Style is somewhere between the Regular Style and the Cursive Style. It became popular thanks to the great calligrapher Wang Xizhi, who lived more than 1,600 years ago. It is said that at the age of seven, Wang Xizhi started practicing calligraphy nonstop and he excelled in all styles. One day, he created a piece of calligraphy called "Preface to the Orchid Pavilion" which is still considered the best Running Style calligraphy in the whole world! (See it on page 75.)

On the next pages are some copies of the works of Wang Xizhi and other calligraphers of ancient China.

Looking at them will help you to see and understand the differences among the five styles.

Seal Style (*zhuan shu*)
Inscriptions on stone cylinders (around 770 B.C.E.)

Seal Style (*zhuan shu*)
Small seal of the Qin era (221–207 B.C.E.)

Clerical Style (*li shu*)
Ode to Shimen (erected in the year 148)

極 河 追
之 南 惟
曰 京 大
魯 韓 古
相 君 華

Clerical Style (*li shu*)
Li Qi Stele (erected in the year 156)

夢僧白晝入其
室摩其頂曰之
當大弘法教言

Regular Style (*kai shu*)
Calligraphy by Liu Gongquan (778–865):
"Xun Mi Tower Stele"

Look at the difference here: the characters written in Regular Style are easy to read, and the ones in the Cursive Style look a little...crazy!

之甘泉不能尚也　誠養神之勝地漢　涼信安體之佳　風徐動有淒清之　金無爨蒸之氣微

Regular Style (*kai shu*)
Calligraphy by Ouyang Xun (557–641):
"The Jiu Cheng Palace"

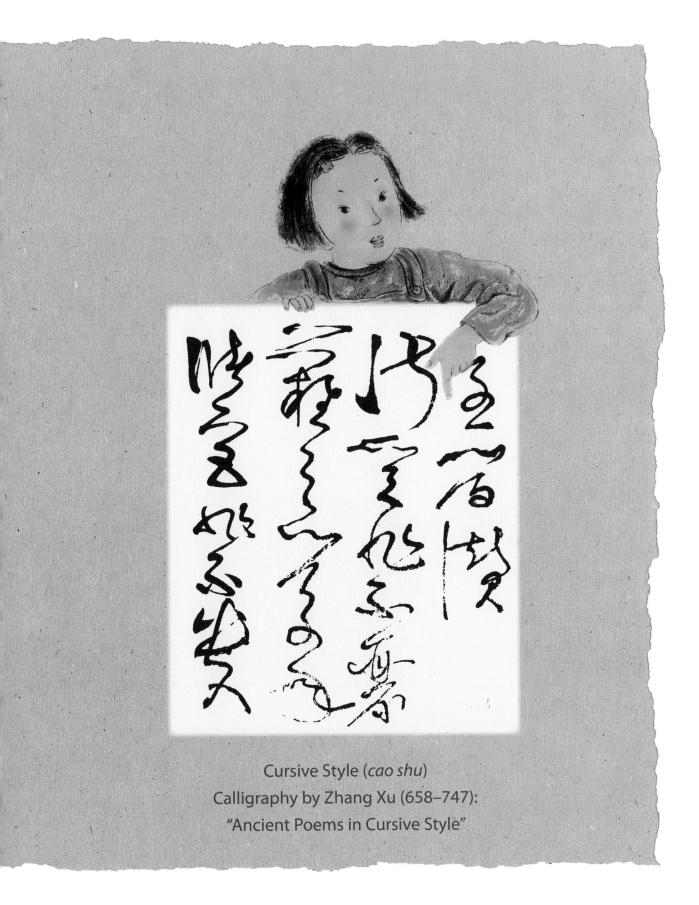

Cursive Style (*cao shu*)
Calligraphy by Zhang Xu (658–747):
"Ancient Poems in Cursive Style"

Cursive Style (*cao shu*)
Copy of calligraphy by Wang Xizhi (307–365):
"Seventeen Books of Models"

Cursive Style (*cao shu*)
Calligraphy by Mi Fu (1052–1108):
"Poems in Cursive Style"

公
贈寧州刺史
孝斌或集事雲
擁花為將或逆

Running Style (*xing shu*)
Calligraphy by Li Yong (678–747):
"General Li Sixun Stele"

永和九年歲在癸丑暮春之初會
于會稽山陰之蘭亭脩禊事
也群賢畢至少長咸集此地
有崇山峻領茂林脩竹又有清流激
湍暎帶左右引以為流觴曲水
列坐其次雖無絲竹管弦之
盛一觴一詠亦足以暢敘幽情
是日也天朗氣清惠風和暢仰

Running Style (*xing shu*)
Copy of calligraphy by Wang Xizhi:
"Preface to the Orchid Pavilion"

The Eight Strokes

With these eight strokes, you can write all the Chinese characters!

They are called the basic strokes, and each is written in a special way. On the illustrations, the path of the brush tip is shown with a thin line to help you see what direction to use. Trace each stroke with your fingertip, to learn it!

In China, they say that to give energy to the strokes and to make them beautiful, the brush needs to "take a running start." The attack—the beginning of the stroke—is that running start. It's a tiny movement, like a loop that just barely turns the point of your brush back over on itself. And the end is when the brush, at the end of the stroke, pulls back a little to stop the energy.

Dian: The dot

To make the dot, first the brush moves up toward the top, then down toward the bottom right. At the end, the tip goes back up left, as if it were turning on itself in order to go back to its starting point.

In China, they say that dots are like the eyebrows of the characters. They have a slightly curved shape.

Heng: The horizontal stroke

In order to gain its "start-up" energy, first the brush loops around the left a tiny bit before going right. This stroke slants upward, instead of being perfectly level. The brush tip stays steady through the middle of the stroke. And to end, the tip loops toward the right before leaving the sheet of paper.

Tiao: The rising stroke

To make this one, your running start is a loop
to the left, then the brush tip goes up in an
angle toward the right, while slowly leaving the
surface of the paper. That makes the stroke end in a point.

Na: Slanting right

The brush makes a loop toward the
left before coming down in a slant
toward the right. The brush tip is
steady in the middle of the stroke,
then you press down more to flatten it, for a wider part. Then
lift the brush up so that the stroke ends in a point.

Pie: Slanting left

The brush makes a loop toward the right
before coming down in a slant toward the
left, in a regular curve. This stroke ends in
a point.

Shù: The vertical stroke

You can make the vertical stroke two different ways. The beginning is the same, but it's the end that changes, so watch carefully! To start, the brush makes a loop toward the right before coming down; the brush tip needs to stay in the middle of the stroke. Then, you choose how to finish:

– You can make a little loop that goes up toward the left; the point is then hidden. This is the "dew drop" vertical stroke.

– Or, you can lift the brush slowly, to get a point that will show. This is the "needle point" vertical stroke.

Gou: The hook

To make the hook, you start it the same as the vertical stroke, *shu*. But you end with a pointy hook that goes up toward the left.

Zhe: The turning stroke

The turning, or broken, stroke is a combination of *heng* and *shu* strokes.

It starts like a horizontal stroke that goes toward the right. But then, you turn the brush to continue the movement downward, without lifting the brush from the paper. It ends like the "dew drop" vertical stroke (on page 81).

Do you remember how to move the brush for each stroke? From the three illustration choices given for each stroke, find the correct one!

Dian

Heng

Tiao

Na

Pie

Zhe

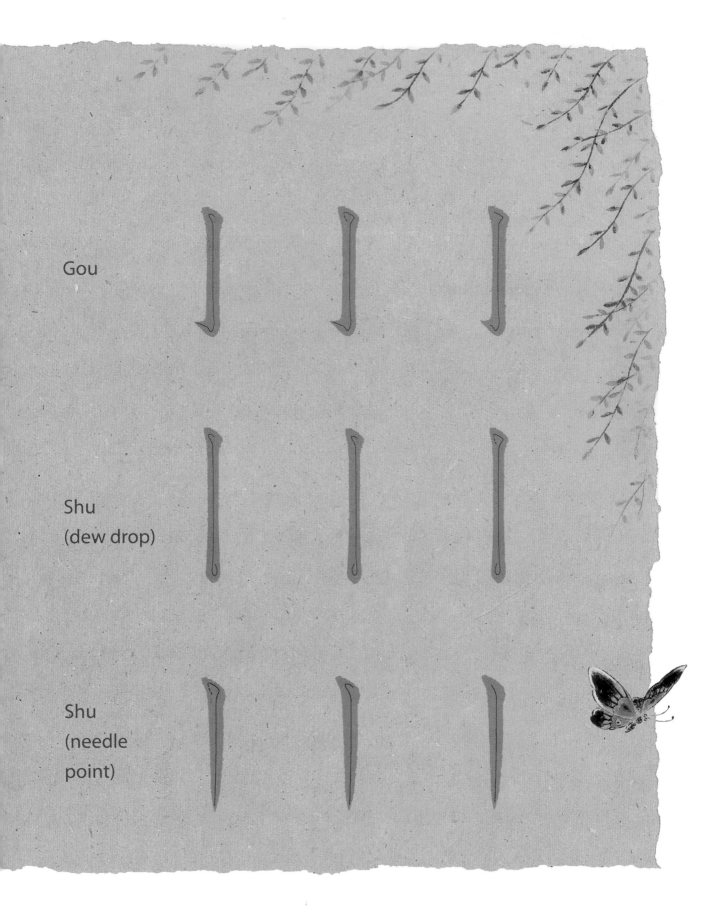

Gou

Shu
(dew drop)

Shu
(needle
point)

Now practice. You can use your fingertip as a pretend brush, tracing the drawings to make each stroke correctly. When you are done, keep on practicing with your brush and ink on more sheets of paper, until you can write them all.

With these eight strokes, you can
write all the characters. It's time to do
some calligraphy!

Writing a Character
in Calligraphy

永

Congratulations! You now know the rules of Chinese writing and the proper position for holding the brush. You know how to recognize the different styles and to write all the strokes. You have tried out your brush, and you've discovered how paper and ink work together.

Now you can put everything you've learned with Mimi to the test: it's your turn to create an entire character, in calligraphy!

- Don't forget that the art of calligraphy is about bringing life and energy to the ink strokes. To do it, you need the power of your mind! Focus your mind before you write a character: try to imagine the character alive on your paper, and when you can see it in your mind, then paint it.

- Remember that imaginary one-size-fits-all square box. Each character takes up the same space, no matter how many strokes it has.

● Write each stroke with a single movement, without lifting the brush from the paper. Be careful, because there's no erasing in calligraphy: if you miss a stroke, you have to redo the whole character.

When you're able to create beautiful characters, you will feel joy, because you'll have acquired a new power!

Look at this character. It means "eternity," and combines almost all the strokes of Chinese calligraphy. Get some ink ready, pick up your brush, and copy it onto your paper. Practice as many times as you want.

永

Practice

On these pages, copy the characters you've learned with Mimi. Don't forget the stroke order, and the path to take for each stroke. And pay attention, because some characters are very similar.

For instance, "earth" 土 and "scholar" 士 are written almost the same way, except that the length of the horizontal strokes is reversed.

And don't confuse "sun" 日 with "eye," 目 which has an extra stroke.

Person

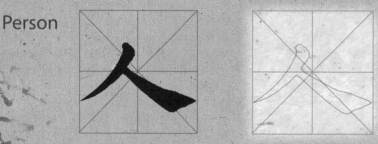

Ten 十

Mouth 口

Sun 日

Eye 目

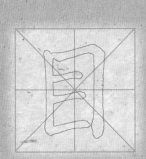
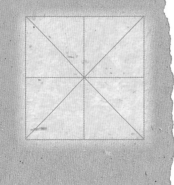

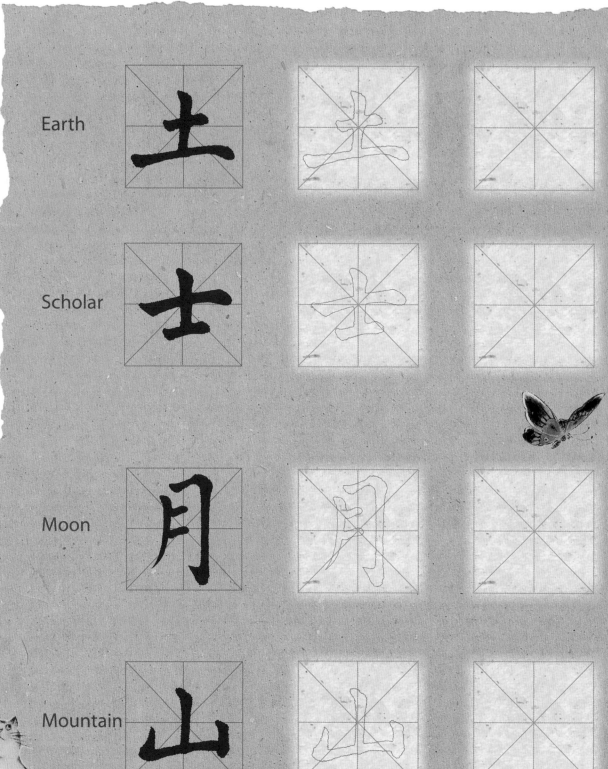

Earth

Scholar

Moon

Mountain

Character	字	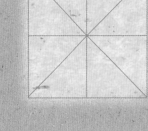	
Eternity	永		
Tiger	虎		
A larger forest	森		

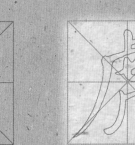

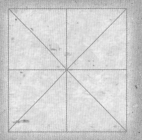

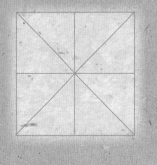

Congratulations! You have reached the end
of your apprenticeship! All the secrets
of Chinese calligraphy have been
revealed to you!

He Zhihong started to draw as a child with
her father, who was a painter. She graduated
from the Beijing Academy of Fine Arts, where
she studied traditional Chinese painting. She
paints—following Chinese tradition—on both silk
and rice paper, and she has also created many
children's books as author and illustrator. She has received the Peter
Pan Award and the Saint-Exupéry Prize.

Guillaume Olive is a Sinologist, which means
that he is an expert on China. He studies
its arts, languages, customs, and history. He
spent many years in China where he met his
wife He Zhihong. He is the author of several
translations of Chinese folktales, ancient
poems, and classic novels. He has won
the Nuit du Livre award and the Saint-Exupéry Prize.

Here are the radicals you'll learn.

A LIST OF RADICALS

Person 亻	Woman 女	Water 氵
Tree 木	Heart 心	Roof 宀
Field 田	Fire 火	Mouth 口
Stone 石	Enclosure 口	Foot 足
Insect 虫	Grass 艹	Hand 扌
Sun 日	Mountain 山